CONSTRUCTION LABORER JOB READINESS ASSESSMENT

Researched and Written by
Norman David Roussell, MBA

Copyright © 2014-2020. All rights reserved.

ISBN 978-0-9796201-5-7

Published by

Use of this assessment does not create an express or implied offer of employment to the assessment taker. In using the assessment, the organization administering the assessment agrees that neither the author nor the publisher is or will be liable or otherwise responsible for any hiring decision made or any action taken or any action not taken due to the use of the assessment. Anyone who uses this assessment, for any purpose, must comply with Title VII of the Civil Rights Act of 1964. Administrators of this assessment should not rely on information provided by this tool as the sole source for any hiring decision. The author specifically disclaims responsibility for any liability, loss or risk incurred directly or indirectly from the contents or use of this assessment. All trade names, trademarks or service marks that appear in this book are trade names, trademarks or service marks of their respective holders and are used in this publication for purposes of description and identification only and do not constitute an endorsement by the author or publisher. This document cannot be reproduced in whole or in part without the written permission of the author.

CONSTRUCTION LABORER JOB READINESS ASSESSMENT

TABLE OF CONTENTS	PAGE
ASSESSMENT-TAKER'S INFORMATION	1
OVERVIEW OF THE ASSESSMENT	3
COMPONENTS OF THE ASSESSMENT	3
ALL ABOUT CONSTRUCTION LABORERS AND HELPERS	4
TIPS ON SUCCESSFULLY COMPLETING THE ASSESSMENT	8
THE ASSESSMENT	
SECTION I- CONSTRUCTION TOOLS AND EQUIPMENT	9
SECTION II- MATH	14
SECTION III- READING COMPREHENSION	16
SECTION IV- CRITICAL THINKING	18
SECTION V- FOLLOWING INSTRUCTIONS	19
SECTION VI- MEASURING LENGTHS	20
SECTION VII- CALCULATING SQUARE FOOTAGE	21
SECTION VIII- CONSTRUCTION TRADES KNOWLEDGE	22
ABOUT CONTRACTOR'S COLLEGE	24

The **Answer Key** and **Results Report** are included in the *CLJRA Facilitator's Guide*.

CONSTRUCTION LABORER JOB READINESS ASSESSMENT

ASSESSMENT TAKER'S INFORMATION

TODAY'S DATE (Month/Day/Year)

NAME (Example: John Q | Doe)
- FIRST/MI
- LAST

PHONE NUMBER(S) (Example: (504) 555-1212)
- CELL
- HOME/OTHER

E-MAIL ADDRESS (Example: johndoe@yahoo.com)

HOME ADDRESS (Example: 1234 Main St., Apt. C, Springfield, USA 54321)
- STREET
- APT./UNIT
- CITY
- STATE
- ZIP

DATE OF BIRTH (Month/Day/Year)

GENDER (Optional)
☐ MALE   ☐ FEMALE   ☐ OTHER

RACE/ETHNICITY (Optional)
☐ BLACK/AFRICAN AMERICAN
☐ WHITE
☐ NATIVE AMERICAN
☐ ASIAN AMERICAN (Specify) _____
☐ LATINO AMERICAN (Specify) _____
☐ PACIFIC ISLANDER (Specify) _____
☐ HISPANIC AMERICAN
☐ MIXED-RACE

1. ARE YOU A U.S. CITIZEN? ☐ YES ☐ NO
2. IF YOU ANSWERED "NO" TO QUESTION 1, ARE YOU AUTHORIZED TO WORK IN THE U.S.? ☐ YES ☐ NO
3. DO YOU HAVE A VALID STATE ISSUED ID? ☐ YES ☐ NO
4. DO YOU HAVE A VALID SOCIAL SECURITY CARD? ☐ YES ☐ NO
5. ARE YOU AN ACTIVE-DUTY MEMBER OR VETERAN OF THE U.S. ARMED FORCES? ☐ YES ☐ NO

DISABILITY STATUS
☐ NONE
☐ DEAF OR SERIOUS DIFFICULTY HEARING
☐ BLIND OR SERIOUS DIFFICULTY SEEING EVEN WHEN WEARING GLASSES
☐ SERIOUS DIFFICULTY WALKING OR CLIMBING STAIRS
☐ OTHER SERIOUS DISABILITY RELATED TO A PHYSICAL, MENTAL OR EMOTIONAL CONDITION (SPECIFY BELOW)

_____
_____

THIS PAGE INTENTIONALLY LEFT BLANK

CONSTRUCTION LABORER JOB READINESS ASSESSMENT

OVERVIEW OF THE ASSESSMENT

The **Construction Laborer Job Readiness Assessment** (Assessment) was developed by Start Smart, LLC's Contractor's College program, to help contractors improve the process of recruiting, hiring and retaining quality U.S. Department of Housing and Urban Development (HUD) Section 3 qualified individuals for work in the construction industry. The assessment is a cognitive examination of the basic knowledge required to work as a construction laborer or helper on a construction site and is designed to identify an individual's strengths, knowledge and skills, as well as their weaknesses, knowledge gaps and skill gaps.

The assessment is a tool that helps test administrators better assist low- and very-income individuals, as well as low-skilled individuals secure employment and training opportunities as they move towards self-sufficiency.

Anyone who uses the CLJRA, for any purpose, must comply with Title VII of the Civil Rights Act of 1964[1] and the Americans with Disability Act.

COMPONENTS OF THE ASSESSMENT

The CLJRA is divided into eight (8) sections and contains 100 questions covering the following topics:

- **Section I- Construction Tools and Equipment (30 questions)**. This section tests an individual's knowledge of commonly used hand tools, power tools and equipment used in construction.
- **Section II- Math (30 questions)**. This section tests an individual's basic math competency in addition, subtraction, multiplication, division, fractions, decimals and percentages.
- **Section III- Reading Comprehension (10 questions)**. This section tests the individual's ability to read, process and understand the context and meaning of a passage.
- **Section IV- Critical Thinking (5 questions)**. This section tests the individual's ability to solve a problem through analysis, reasoning and logic.
- **Section V- Following Instructions (1 question)**. This section tests the individual's ability to follow instructions.
- **Section VI- Measuring Lengths (4 questions)**. This section tests the individual's competency with measuring and properly recording different lengths using a ruler or measuring tape.
- **Section VII- Calculating Square Footage (5 questions)**. This section tests the individual's ability to utilize the measurements on a blueprint to calculate the square footage of a building.
- **Section VIII- Construction Trades Knowledge (15 questions)**. This section tests the individual's basic knowledge of major construction trades and construction site safety.

---

[1] Visit www.eeoc.gov for guidance and requirements for complying with Title VII of the Civil Rights Act of 1964.

CONSTRUCTION LABORER JOB READINESS ASSESSMENT

ALL ABOUT CONSTRUCTION LABORERS AND HELPERS[2]

Construction laborers and helpers perform many basic tasks that require physical labor on commercial and residential construction sites including, but not limited to:

- Cleaning and preparing construction sites by removing debris and possible hazards
- Loading or unloading building materials to be used in construction
- Building or taking apart bracing, scaffolding, and temporary structures
- Digging trenches, backfilling holes, or compacting earth to prepare for construction
- Operating or tending equipment and machines used in construction
- Helping craft workers with their duties
- Following construction plans and instructions from supervisors or more experienced workers

Construction laborers and helpers work on almost all construction sites, performing a wide range of tasks from the very easy to the extremely difficult and hazardous. Although many of the tasks they perform require some training and experience, most require little skill and can be learned quickly.

Construction Laborers

Construction laborers perform a variety of construction-related activities during all phases of construction. However, the main task laborers perform is preparing and cleaning up construction sites. Although most laborers are generalists- such as those who install barricades, cones and markers to control traffic patterns- many others specialize. For example, those who operate the machines that pour concrete or asphalt on roads are more likely to specialize in those areas.

Most construction laborers work in the following areas:

- Building homes and businesses
- Tearing down buildings
- Removing hazardous materials
- Building highways and roads
- Digging tunnels and mine shafts

Construction laborers use a variety of tools and equipment. Some tools are simple, such as brooms and shovels; other equipment is more sophisticated, such as pavement breakers, jackhammers, earth tampers and surveying equipment.

With special training, laborers may help transport and use explosives or run hydraulic boring machines to dig out tunnels. They may learn to use laser beam equipment to place pipes and use computers to control robotic pipe cutters. They may also become certified to remove asbestos, lead, chemicals of other hazardous materials.

---

[2] Sources: www.bls.gov and www.dol.gov. The information was edited for this publication.

Helpers

Helpers assist construction craft workers, such as electricians and carpenters, with a variety of basic tasks. They may carry tools and materials or help set up equipment. For example, many helpers work with cement masons to move and set forms (molds that determine the shape of concrete). Many other helpers assist with taking apart equipment, cleaning up sites, and disposing of waste, as well as helping with any other needs of craft workers.

Many construction trades have helpers who assist craft workers. The following are trades that have associated helpers:

- **Brickmasons, Blockmasons and Stonemasons**
  Brickmasons, blockmasons and stonemasons (or, simply, masons) use bricks, concrete blocks and natural and man-made stones to build fences, walkways, walls and other structures.

- Carpenters
  Carpenters construct and repair building frameworks and structures—such as stairways, doorframes, partitions and rafters—made from wood and other materials. They also may install kitchen cabinets, siding and drywall.

- Electricians
  Electricians install and maintain electrical power, communications, lighting and control systems in homes, businesses, and factories.

- Painters- Construction and Maintenance
  Painters apply paint, stain, and coatings to walls, buildings, bridges and other structures.

- Plumbers, Pipefitters, and Steamfitters
  Plumbers, pipefitters, and steamfitters install and repair pipes that carry liquids or gases to and in businesses, homes and factories.

- Roofers
  Roofers repair and install the roofs of buildings using a variety of materials, including shingles, asphalt and metal.

- Tile and Marble Setters; Floor Layers (General)
  Tile and marble setters apply hard tile and marble to walls, floors and other surfaces. Floor layers install carpet, wood floors and laminate tiles in structures.

- Hazardous Materials Removal Workers
  Hazardous materials (hazmat) removal workers identify and dispose of asbestos, radioactive and nuclear waste, arsenic, lead and other hazardous materials. They also neutralize and clean up materials that are flammable, corrosive, reactive or toxic.

CONSTRUCTION LABORER JOB READINESS ASSESSMENT

Work Environment
Most construction laborers and helpers do physically demanding work. Some work at great heights or outdoors in all weather conditions; others may be required to work in tunnels. They must use earplugs around loud equipment and wear gloves, safety glasses, and other protective gear.

Injuries and Illnesses
Construction laborers have one of the highest rates of injuries and illnesses of all occupations. Workers may experience cuts from materials and tools, falls from ladders and scaffolding, and burns from chemicals or equipment. Some jobs expose workers to harmful materials, fumes, odors, or dangerous machinery. Workers also may experience muscle fatigue and injuries related to lifting and carrying heavy materials. Although they face similar hazards, construction helpers generally experience a rate of injuries and illnesses that is close to the national average.

Work Schedules
Like many construction workers, most laborers and helpers work full time. Although they sometimes stop work because of bad weather, they often work overtime to meet deadlines. Laborers and helpers on highway and bridge projects often work overnight to avoid major disruptions to traffic. In some parts of the country, construction laborers and helpers may work only during certain seasons.

Education
Although there are no specific education requirements, high school classes in English, mathematics, blueprint reading, welding, and shop can be helpful. Some workers attend a trade or vocational school, an association training class, or community college to receive further training.

Training
Most construction laborers and helpers learn through short-term on-the-job training after being hired by a construction contractor or a temporary-help employment agency. Workers typically gain experience by doing jobs under the guidance of experienced workers.

Although the majority of workers learn by assisting experienced workers, some choose to attend apprenticeship programs. Apprenticeship programs generally include 2 to 4 years of technical instruction and on-the-job training.

Workers learn basic construction skills, such as communication, blueprint reading, proper tools and equipment use, and safety and health procedures. The remainder of the curriculum consists of specialized skills training in three of the largest segments of the construction industry: building construction, heavy and highway construction, and environmental remediation for removing such materials as lead or asbestos.

Several groups, including unions and contractor associations, sponsor apprenticeship programs. Apprenticeship programs usually have only a basic age qualification—age 18 or older—for entrance. A high school diploma or equivalent is preferred but not required.

Licenses, Certifications, and Registrations

Laborers who remove hazardous materials (hazmat) must have a federal hazmat license required for all hazardous materials removal workers. Depending on the work they do, other laborers may also need specific certifications. The following are examples of areas which may require certification:

- Asbestos removal
- Energy auditing
- Lead abatement
- OSHA 10 and/or 30-hour Construction Safety Certification
- Pipeline operation
- Radiological work
- Rough terrain forklift operation
- Scaffold use and building
- Signaling
- Weatherization
- Welding
- Work zone safety

Advancement

Through experience and training, construction laborers can advance into positions that involve more complex tasks. For example, laborers may earn certifications in welding, scaffold erecting, or concrete finishing and then spend more time performing activities that require the specialized skill. Through training and experience, helpers can potentially move into construction craft occupations. For example, experience as a helper may lead to becoming a tilesetter.

Important Qualities

Color vision. Laborers and helpers may need to be able to distinguish colors to do their job. For example, an electrician's helper must be able to distinguish different colors of wire to help an electrician.

Math skills. Laborers and some helpers need to perform basic math calculations to do their job. They often help with measuring on jobsites or they may be part of a surveying crew.

Mechanical skills. Laborers frequently are required to operate and maintain equipment, such as jackhammers.

Physical stamina and strength. Laborers and helpers must have endurance to perform strenuous tasks throughout the day. Highway laborers, for example, can spend hours on their feet with few breaks. Laborers and helpers must often lift heavy materials or equipment. For example, cement mason helpers must move cinder blocks, which weigh more than 40 pounds each.

CONSTRUCTION LABORER JOB READINESS ASSESSMENT

Tips on Successfully Completing the Assessment

Tip #1
Read the instructions for each section carefully **BEFORE** you begin answering the questions.

Tip #2
If you have any questions, ask the Test Administrator for assistance **BEFORE** you begin each section.

Tip #3
Answer every question, even if you are unsure of the answer.

CONSTRUCTION LABORER JOB READINESS ASSESSMENT

SECTION I- CONSTRUCTION TOOLS AND EQUIPMENT

Instructions: Match the NAME OF THE TOOL with the correct PICTURE OF THE TOOL by placing the number that is next to the name of the tool in the box with the picture of the tool.

For example,

1. Pliers   2. Hammer   3. Heavy Duty Stapler

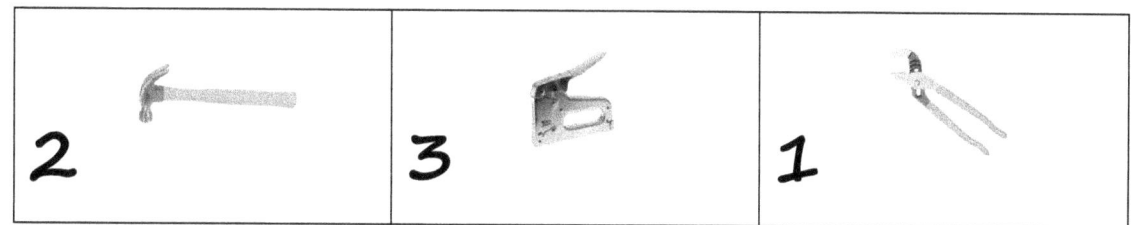

Good luck!

THIS PAGE INTENTIONALLY LEFT BLANK

CONSTRUCTION LABORER JOB READINESS ASSESSMENT

1. HARD HAT
2. ADJUSTABLE WRENCH
3. FLASHLIGHT
4. POWER DRILL
5. SHOVEL
6. COMBINATION WRENCH
7. CAULKING GUN
8. MEASURING TAPE
9. PRESSURE WASHER
10. CIRCULAR SAW
11. MASONRY TROWEL
12. HAND SAW

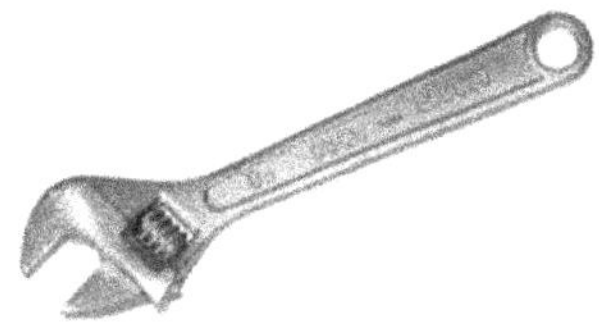

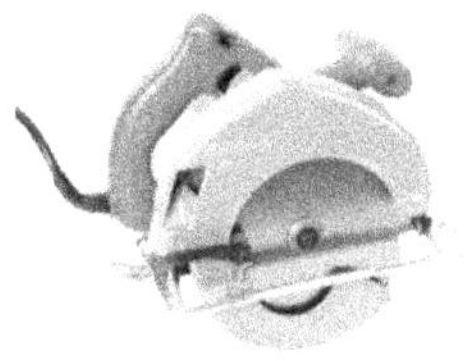

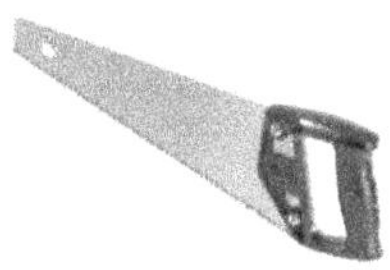

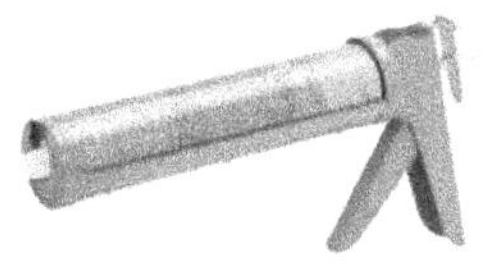

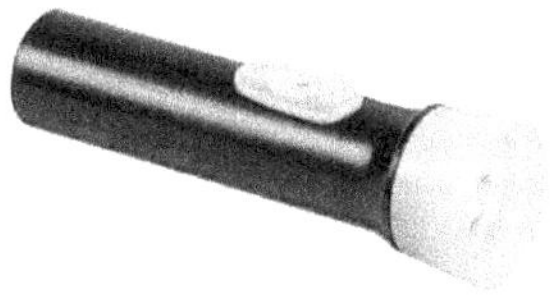

CONSTRUCTION LABORER JOB READINESS ASSESSMENT

13. PLASTERER'S TROWEL
14. WIRE STRIPPER
15. SAFETY GOGGLES
16. LEVEL
17. SOCKET WRENCHES
18. BELT SANDER
19. NAIL GUN
20. PAINT SCRAPER
21. SCREWDRIVER
22. PAINT BRUSH
23. HEX KEY OR ALLEN WRENCH SET
24. PIPE WRENCH

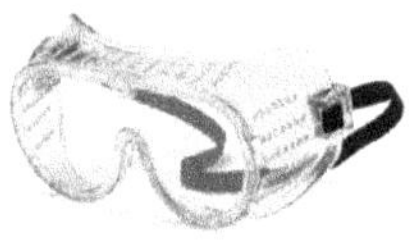

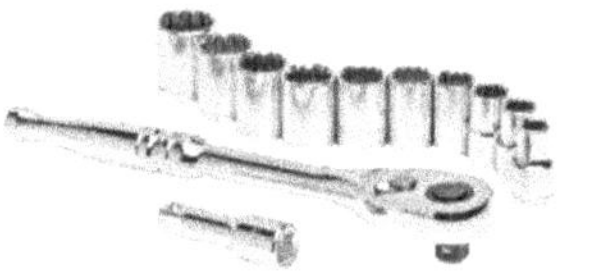

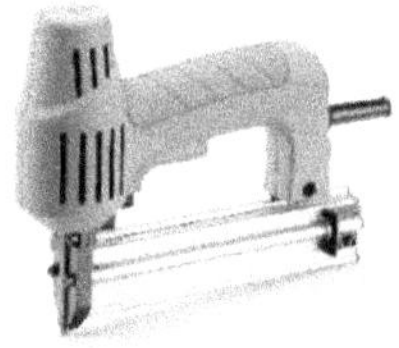

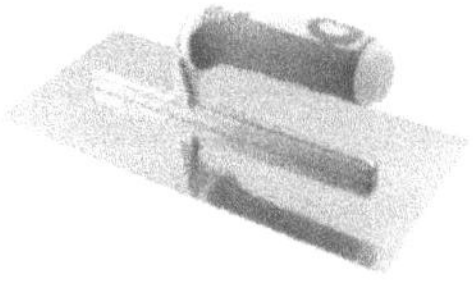

CONSTRUCTION LABORER JOB READINESS ASSESSMENT

25. DUMP TRUCK   26. SCAFFOLD   27. CONCRETE MIXER TRUCK
28. ROLL OFF CONTAINER 29. CRAWLER CRANE   30. BULLDOZER

CONSTRUCTION LABORER JOB READINESS ASSESSMENT

SECTION II - MATH

Instructions: Circle the correct answer under columns A-D to the right of the question. You can use the blank pages provided at the end of the assessment to calculate your answers if necessary.

Example	A	B	C	D
1) 120 + 30 =	180	(150)	200	165

Addition	A	B	C	D
1) 380 + 20	390	410	400	440
2) 100 + 50	150	175	160	120
3) 575 + 15	580	610	620	590
4) 109 + 27	135	147	136	149
5) 648 + 13	651	661	683	678

Subtraction	A	B	C	D
6) 450 - 50	500	400	350	450
7) 165 - 15	110	180	175	150
8) 330 - 35	305	310	295	280
9) 219 - 13	206	216	232	246
10) 864 - 551	1,315	313	465	321

Multiplication	A	B	C	D
11) 10 x 5 =	15	60	55	50
12) 8 x 8 =	66	64	88	84
13) 10 x 12 =	120	112	102	122
14) 34 x 0 =	34	340	0	38
15) 15 x 3 =	30	45	35	60

Division	A	B	C	D
16) 100 ÷ 50 =	50	2	15	10
17) 250 ÷ 10 =	15	20	25	12
18) 408 ÷ 4 =	110	84	148	102
19) 321 ÷ 3 =	107	103	113	121

Fractions	A	B	C	D
20) ¼ + ¾ =	1	5/4	2/4	4/8
21) ½ + ⅓ =	2/6	5/6	1/6	3/6
22) ⅞ − ⅜ =	8/10	2/8	4/8	10/8

Decimals	A	B	C	D
23) 1.8 + 2.1 =	4.1	3.9	3.0	3.7
24) 10.5 + 5.3 =	15.8	13.5	15.0	10.53
25) 126.53 − 12.51 =	114.02	115.52	111.31	112.03

Percentages. Convert the following numbers to their corresponding percentages.

Examples: 0.15 = 15% and ¾ = 75%.

26) 0.25 = _____ %

27) 0.38 = _____ %

28) 1/2 = _____ %

29) 2/3 = _____ %

30) 0.125 = _____ %

CONSTRUCTION LABORER JOB READINESS ASSESSMENT

SECTION III- READING COMPREHENSION

Instructions: Read the two passages, *The Construction Industry* and *Women in Construction*, and answer the questions that follow.

PASSAGE #1: THE CONSTRUCTION INDUSTRY

The construction industry[3] includes a wide range of professions all engaged in the process of building new structures and altering, repair or renovating existing structures. Some examples of construction industry projects include:

- Building new single-family homes or renovating existing single-family homes;
- Building and repairing bridges, streets, roads and highways;
- Building and altering commercial office buildings, apartment complexes and shopping malls; and
- Building new schools and renovating existing schools.

Some of the major professions involved in the construction industry during the pre-construction phase, include architects, engineers and demolition contractors. Some of the professions, also known as trades, involved during the construction phase include carpenters, electricians, plumbers and masons (a mason is also known as a bricklayer). According to the U.S. Census Bureau's *Value of Construction Put in Place Survey*, in March 2014, the monthly estimate of the dollar value of construction work being done in the U.S. was over $942 billion.

1. The construction industry includes a wide range of professions.
    a. True
    b. False

2. Examples of construction industry projects include:
    a. Renovating single family homes
    b. Building new schools
    c. Building and repairing bridges
    d. All of the above

3. An electrician performs work during the construction phase of a project.
    a. False
    b. True

4. All of the following are typical construction industry trades, except:
    a. Carpenter
    b. Electrician
    c. Pilot
    d. Plumber

5. According to the U.S. Census Bureau's *Value of Construction Put in Place Survey*, in March 2014, the monthly estimate of the dollar value of construction work being done in the U.S. was over _____ dollars.
    a. $500 million
    b. $942 billion
    c. $10 million

---

[3] Sources: www.osha.gov, www.census.gov and www.dol.gov

CONSTRUCTION LABORER JOB READINESS ASSESSMENT

PASSAGE #2: WOMEN IN CONSTRUCTION

The number of women employed in the U.S. construction industry grew by 81.3% from 1985 to 2007[4]; however, due to a loss of over 2.5 million constructions jobs during the recession of 2007 to 2010, more than 300,000 women left the construction industry by 2010.

While only 9% of all U.S. construction workers are women, there were still over 800,000 women workers employed in construction in 2010. The majority of women working in construction work in managerial, professional, administrative and production occupations. Approximately 200,000 women were employed as laborers, electricians, plumbers and other trades.

1. The construction industry lost over _____ jobs during the recession of 2007 to 2010.

    a. 1 million
    b. 1.5 million
    c. 5 million
    d. 2.5 million

2. The number of women employed in the construction industry declined from 1985 to 2007.

    a. True
    b. False

3. _____ 10% of all U.S. construction workers are women.

    a. Less than
    b. More than
    c. Exactly

4. The majority of women working in construction work in managerial, professional, administrative and production occupations.

    a. True
    b. False

5. _____ 300,000 women had left the construction industry by 2010 as a result of the recession that began in 2007.

    a. Exactly
    b. Less than
    c. More than

---

[4] Source: www.census.gov

CONSTRUCTION LABORER JOB READINESS ASSESSMENT

SECTION IV- CRITICAL THINKING

Instructions: Answer the following questions.

1. What numbers comes next in this sequence: 2, 4, 6, 8, ___, 12, 14, 16, ___, 20.

    a. 9 and 18
    b. 10 and 18
    c. 11 and 17
    d. 10 and 19

2. A **square** has ___ sides, a **triangle** as ___ sides and an **octagon** has ___ sides.

    a. 4, 3, and 5
    b. 3, 4, and 6
    c. 4, 3, and 8
    d. 4, 3, and 6

3. How long will it take for you to drive from New York to Boston and return home to New York if it takes four (4) hours to drive from New York to Boston and you add a half-hour (30-minutes) to stop for gas and rest each way?

    a. 9 hours
    b. 10 hours
    c. 8 hours
    d. 11 hours

    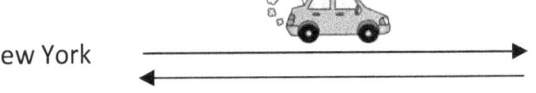

    New York — Boston

    4 hours travel + 30-minutes to stop for gas and rest each way

4. **Hand** is to **glove** as:

    a. Head is to scarf
    b. Foot is to shoe
    c. Belt is to waist
    d. Leg is to arm

    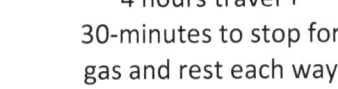

5. If your car's gas tank holds ten (10) gallons and your car averages twenty (20) miles per gallon, how many miles can your car travel on a tank of gas?

    a. 100 miles
    b. 150 miles
    c. 300 miles
    d. 200 miles

    Hint: 3 gallons x 20 miles per gallon = 60 miles

CONSTRUCTION LABORER JOB READINESS ASSESSMENT

SECTION V- FOLLOWING INSTRUCTIONS

Instructions: Read every question before you answer any of the questions.

1. How old will you be in five years? _____

2. What is your favorite color? _____

3. What is your favorite professional sports team?
   _____

4. Who is your favorite actor or actress?
   _____

5. Who is your favorite musician or musical group?
   _____

6. What is your favorite TV show (past or present)?
   _____

7. Who was the first President of the United States of America?
   _____

8. What is your favorite hobby or activity to do when you are not at work?
   _____

9. Do not answer numbers 1-8. Only follow the instructions for questions 9 and 10.

10. Print your full name in the box below.

SECTION VI- MEASURING LENGTHS

Instructions: Using the diagram of the ruler below, identify the measurements indicated.

For example, $2^{15/16}$ inches

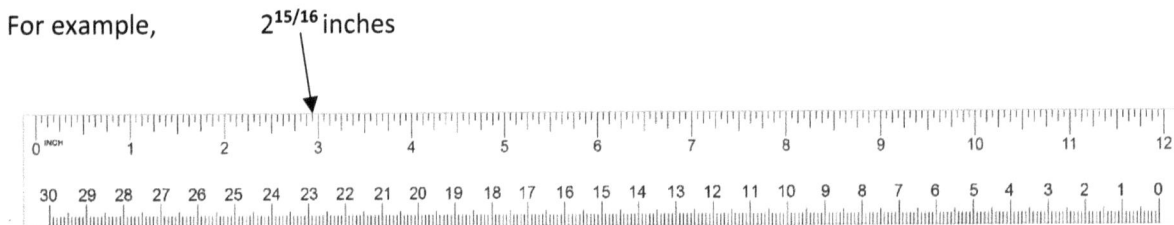

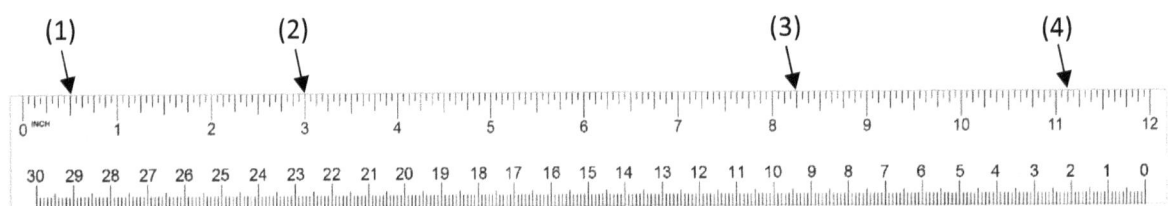

(1) _____

(2) _____

(3) _____

(4) _____

CONSTRUCTION LABORER JOB READINESS ASSESSMENT

SECTION VII- CALCULATING SQUARE FOOTAGE

Instructions: Calculate the total living area (square footage) of the home pictured below using the room dimensions provided in the diagram. DO NOT INCLUDE THE ENTRY WAY AND CLOSET IN YOUR CALCULATION. For example,

Room	Dimensions	Square Footage
Bedroom dimensions	10' x 10'	100 sq. ft.
Living room dimensions	12' x 10'	120 sq. ft.
Total Square Footage		**220 sq. ft.**

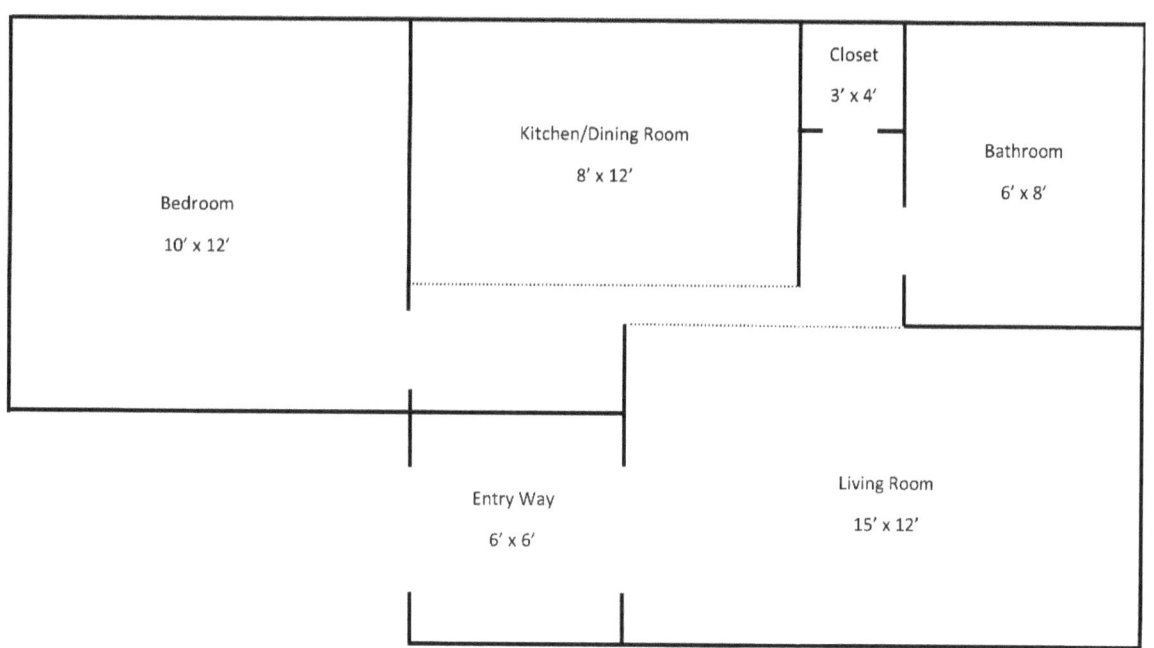

Calculate your answers in the space below
(You can use the blank pages provided at the end of the assessment to calculate your answers)

Room	Dimensions	Square Footage
Bedroom	10' x 12'	
Kitchen/Dining Room	8' x 12'	
Bathroom	6' x 8'	
Living Room	15' x 12'	
Total Square Footage		

CONSTRUCTION LABORER JOB READINESS ASSESSMENT

SECTION VIII- CONSTRUCTION TRADES KNOWLEDGE

Instructions: Choose the correct answer from the choices provided.

1. A mason uses bricks, concrete blocks and natural and man-made stones to build walls, fences, walkways and other structures.

   a. True
   b. False

2. Concrete is made by mixing _____, _____, _____ and _____.

   a. Water, oil, rocks and sand
   b. Concrete, sand, mortar and gravel
   c. Cement, sand, aggregate and water
   d. Sand, rocks, oil and water

3. _____ construct and repair building frameworks and structures made from wood and other materials.

   a. Carpenters
   b. Masons
   c. Plumbers
   d. Musicians

4. The amount of roofing material needed to cover 100 sq. ft. is called a _____.

   a. Case
   b. Square
   c. Box
   d. Carton

5. The toehold on a scaffold is used to _____.

   a. Help prevent tools from falling
   b. Provide a place to put your feet when standing on a scaffold
   c. Add stability to the scaffold
   d. Connect two scaffolds together

6. Who is responsible for maintain a safe and healthy working environment on a construction site?

   a. General contractor
   b. Subcontractors
   c. Workers
   d. All of the above

7. If a square of roofing material covers 100 sq. ft., how many squares will it take to cover a roof that is 800 sq. ft.?

   a. 10
   b. 8
   c. 16
   d. 5

8. Plumbers install and repair pipes and fixtures that carry liquids or gases to and in homes, businesses and other structures.

    a. True
    b. False

9. It is best to use a polyester or nylon bristle paint brush with _____ based paints.

    a. Varnish
    b. Oil
    c. Water
    d. Liquid

10. First aid kits on a construction job site should be checked every week.

    a. True
    b. False

11. A "P-Trap" is used in:

    a. Carpentry
    b. Masonry
    c. Plumbing
    d. Painting

12. An _____ installs and maintains electrical power, communications, lighting and control systems in homes, businesses and other structures.

    a. Painter
    b. Electrician
    c. Plumber
    d. Architect

13. Carpenters use marking tools, like pencils, to ensure they are cutting wood or other materials accurately.

    a. True
    b. False

14. An electrician uses a _____ to determine whether there is current flowing through a wire and to test for proper grounding.

    a. Metal rod
    b. Finger
    c. Voltage tester (Voltmeter)
    d. Light switch

15. Painters regularly use all of the following tools except:

    a. Drop cloth
    b. Pipe wrench
    c. Paint roller
    d. Caulking gun

CONSTRUCTION LABORER JOB READINESS ASSESSMENT

ABOUT CONTRACTOR'S COLLEGE

Contractor's College is an industry-focused, award-winning construction business management training program designed to help small, minority- and women-owned construction and professional services firms ("emerging firms") compete in the highly competitive multi-billion-dollar a year U.S. construction industry. Contractor's College teaches program participants how to improve their businesses in the four major areas of consideration of project owners, prime contractors, procurement officers, banks, insurance and surety companies:

Credit, Capacity, Capital and Credibility.

Since 2006, state and local government agencies, Fortune 500 corporations, universities and non-profit organizations have chosen Contractor's College to train business owners in their communities on how to build more credible, competitive and higher-performing businesses positioned for success in the construction industry.

The overarching objective of Contractor's College is to help emerging firms become qualified and prepared to bid and perform on large public- and private-sector construction projects. Additional objectives include:

- Improving the business knowledge, strategy and management skills of emerging business owners;
- Increasing the financing and bonding capacity of participating firms; and
- Providing participants an opportunity to network with public- and private-sector stakeholders to discuss opportunities in the construction industry.

Contractor's College at-a-glance:

- ✓ Award-winning training program
- ✓ Over 14-years of educating construction industry professionals
- ✓ Over 850 program graduates
- ✓ Over 4,200 workshop attendees
- ✓ Over $150 million in surety bonding secured by graduates
- ✓ Over $220 million in contracts secured by graduates

Learn more:

www.ContractorsCollege.com

THIS PAGE INTENTIONALLY LEFT BLANK

THIS PAGE INTENTIONALLY LEFT BLANK

www.ingramcontent.com/pod-product-compliance
Lightning Source LLC
Chambersburg PA
CBHW080555170426
43195CB00016B/2796